Fact Finders™

Questions and Answers: Countries

# North Korea

## A Question and Answer Book

by Susan E. Haberle

Consultant:
Dr. Leonid A. Petrov
Instructor, Intercultural Institute of California
San Francisco, California

Capstone
press

Mankato, Minnesota

Fact Finders is published by Capstone Press,
151 Good Counsel Drive, P.O. Box 669, Mankato, Minnesota 56002.
www.capstonepress.com

*Library of Congress Cataloging-in-Publication Data*
Haberle, Susan E.
    North Korea: a question and answer book / by Susan E. Haberle.
    p. cm.—(Fact finders. Questions and answers. Countries)
    Includes bibliographical references and index.
    ISBN 0-7368-3756-6 (hardcover)
    1. Korea (North)—Juvenile literature. 2. Korea (North) I. Title. II. Series.
DS932.2.H33 2005
951.93—dc22                                                          2004009812

Summary: Describes the geography, history, economy, and culture of North Korea in a
    simple question-and-answer format.

**Editorial Credits**
Donald Lemke, editor; Kia Adams, set designer; Kate Opseth, book designer; Nancy Steers,
    map illustrator; Wanda Winch, photo researcher; Scott Thoms, photo editor

**Photo Credits**
Art Directors/Jane Sweeney, cover (background), 9; AP/Wide World Photos/World Food
Program, 16; Atlas/Ozcan Yuksek, 1, 4; Bruce Coleman Inc./Norman Owen Tomalin, 20;
Corbis/NewSport/Mitchell Layton, 18–19; Corbis/Reuters/Lee Jae-Won, 13, 27;
Corbis/Reuters/Toshiyuki Aizawa, 8; Corbis/Tom Haskell, cover (foreground); Corbis
Sygma/Joren Gerhard, 23; Craig J. Brown, 24–25; The Image Works/Visum/Sintesi, 15;
Panos Pictures/Dermot Tatlow, 10–11; Panos Pictures/Jeremy Horner, 17; Photo courtesy of
Dan Drew, 29 (coins); Photo courtesy of Dr. Leonid A. Petrov, 21; Photo courtesy of Richard
Sutherland, 29 (bill); Ronald de Hommel, 6–7; StockHaus Ltd., 29 (flag)

**Artistic Effects**
Ingram Publishing, 12

1 2 3 4 5 6 10 09 08 07 06 05

# Table of Contents

# Where is North Korea?

North Korea is a small country in eastern Asia. It is located on the northern half of the Korean Peninsula. The country is slightly smaller than the U.S. state of New York.

Most of North Korea is covered with mountains. Mount Paektu is the tallest peak. It is on North Korea's border with China.

*Mountains and hills cover much of North Korea.* ➤

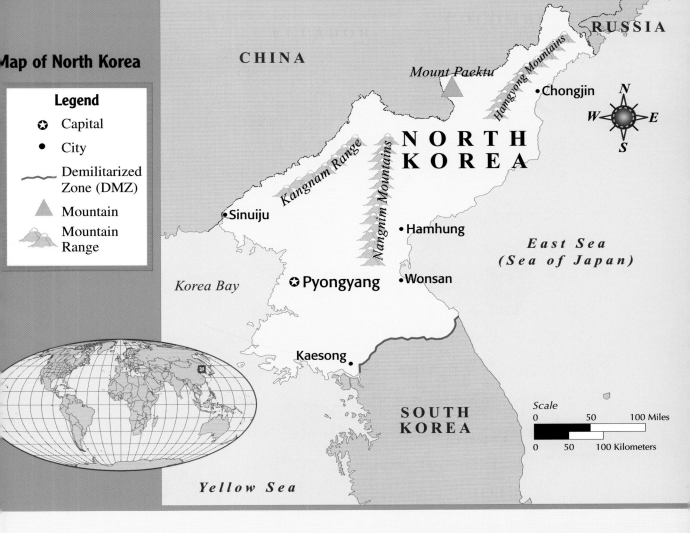

Map of North Korea

**Legend**

| | |
|---|---|
| ✪ | Capital |
| ● | City |
| ∿ | Demilitarized Zone (DMZ) |
| ▲ | Mountain |
| ⛰ | Mountain Range |

CHINA

RUSSIA

Mount Paektu

Hamgyong Mountains

Chongjin

**NORTH KOREA**

N
W E
S

Kangnam Range

Nangnim Mountains

Sinuiju

Hamhung

East Sea (Sea of Japan)

Korea Bay

✪ Pyongyang

Wonsan

Kaesong

SOUTH KOREA

Scale

0    50    100 Miles

0    50    100 Kilometers

Yellow Sea

Deep valleys and small plains are other landforms in North Korea. Valleys divide the mountains across the central part of the country. Plains cover much of the coasts. Most North Koreans live in these valleys and plains.

# When did North Korea become a country?

North Korea became a country on September 9, 1948. Before then, North and South Korea were one country called Korea. Japan ruled Korea from 1910 to 1945.

After World War II (1939–1945), Russia controlled the northern half of Korea. The United States controlled the southern part. Three years later, both North and South Korea became **independent** countries.

## Fact!

Large families called dynasties ruled early Korea. The Choson dynasty ruled from 1392 to 1910. North Koreans still call their country Choson.

*Soldiers guard the Demilitarized Zone between North and South Korea.*

On June 25, 1950, North Korea attacked South Korea. This action started the Korean War (1950–1953). After three years, the countries stopped fighting. They built a middle ground called the Demilitarized Zone (DMZ). This border area still separates the two countries.

# What type of government does North Korea have?

North Korea is a **communist** country. The government owns all of the land, houses, and businesses. People in North Korea have few rights. This system is different from the U.S. government. In the United States, people can own houses, earn money, and elect leaders.

*Kim Jong Il became the leader of North Korea in 1994.* ▶

*People visit a statue of former leader Kim Il Sung. Although Kim died in 1994, he remains North Korea's official president.*

The Korean Workers' Party (KWP) rules North Korea. The head of the KWP is elected by the Supreme People's Assembly. Each of the 687 assembly members serves a four-year term. During this time, they help pass laws approved by the KWP.

# What kind of housing does North Korea have?

North Koreans have many types of housing. Government workers often live in two-story homes or large apartments. Most other workers live in smaller houses and apartments. Outside the cities, farmers live in older homes with thatched roofs. They often share these homes with other families.

**Where do people in North Korea live?**

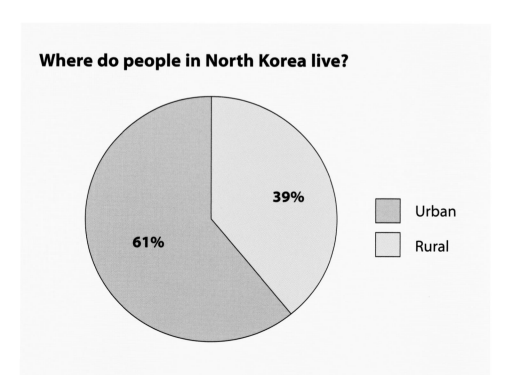

39%

61%

Urban

Rural

*Many North Koreans live in crowded apartment buildings.*

Most people in Pyongyang and other cities live in high-rise apartments. Some apartment buildings are 40 floors tall. Most apartments have TVs, refrigerators, and furniture.

# What are North Korea's forms of transportation?

North Koreans use many forms of transportation. In cities, they travel by subway, bus, **tram**, or bicycle. In small villages, they often ride in oxcarts or walk.

North Koreans need permission to travel to cities near the country's borders. Soldiers often patrol roads to these areas. They stop and check cars that pass by.

## Fact!

*Most North Koreans do not travel at night. The country does not make enough electricity to light street lamps.*

*In Pyongyang and other cities, people often bike or walk to work.*

Pyongyang has a small airport. North Koreans must have permission to travel outside of their country. Visitors from other countries cannot travel within North Korea alone. They must hire a guide to take them places.

# What are North Korea's major industries?

Mining and **manufacturing** are important to North Korea. The government controls both of these industries. North Koreans mine coal, lead, iron ore, copper, and gold. From these **minerals**, workers make machinery and **military** products. Some goods are shipped to nearby countries.

| What does North Korea import and export? | |
|---|---|
| **Imports** | **Exports** |
| grains | military products |
| machinery | minerals |
| petroleum | textiles |

*Some North Koreans make machinery at factories.*

Many North Koreans also fish along the country's coastal waters. Fishers catch and sell pollack, sardines, squid, and mackerel.

# What is school like in North Korea?

All North Korean children must finish 11 years of school, including one year of kindergarten. After kindergarten, students go to four years of grade school. Then they attend six years of secondary school.

*Grade school students in North Korea wear uniforms to school.* ➤

*Students in North Korea learn traditional songs in music classes.*

North Korean students study many subjects, including language, math, and music. Students also have classes on politics and government. They learn to respect the rules and leaders of their country.

# What are North Korea's favorite sports and games?

Soccer is the national sport of North Korea. The country has a men's team and a women's team. Many children enjoy watching and playing soccer with friends.

Tae kwon do is another popular sport. Tae kwon do is a form of **martial arts** that began in Korea. North Korean children often learn tae kwon do when they are young.

## Fact!

*Since 2000, athletes from North and South Korea have marched together in the opening ceremonies of the Olympics.*

*A North Korean soccer player goes for the ball during a World Cup match against Nigeria.*

North Koreans enjoy other sports and games. Some people climb and hike in the country's mountains. Others compete at table tennis. They also play a game with four sticks called *yut*. Players throw the sticks into the air. The way the sticks land shows players where to move on a game board.

# What are the traditional art forms in North Korea?

North Korea is famous for beautiful handwriting called **calligraphy**. Artists draw or paint symbols with long, flowing strokes. These symbols usually stand for words. Painting and **ceramic** pottery are also popular.

Many North Koreans enjoy playing music. They perform folk music with stringed instruments, bamboo flutes, and drums.

*Large paintings in North Korea honor the country's leaders.* ▶

*Many North Korean children enjoy painting.*

Today, most art in North Korea is controlled by the government. Many artists make statues, sculptures, and paintings of government leaders. They write books, plays, and songs that honor their leaders.

# What major holidays do North Koreans celebrate?

North Koreans honor their most popular leaders, Kim Il Sung and Kim Jong Il. Their birthdays are the country's grandest holidays. People watch parades and gymnastic shows. They visit family members and eat special foods.

People in North Korea celebrate other national holidays. September 9 is Democratic People's Republic of Korea Foundation Day. This day marks when North Korea became a country.

## What other holidays do people in North Korea celebrate?

*Constitution Day*
*Fatherland Liberation War Victory Day*
*May Day*
*Workers' Party Foundation Day*

*On April 1, 1992, people gathered at a large stadium for Kim Il Sung's 80th birthday. Each person held up a colored card to make a giant picture.*

North Koreans do not celebrate many religious or seasonal holidays. Most people in the country are not religious. In the past, the government banned seasonal celebrations. Today, North Koreans enjoy Lunar New Year's Day and a day of thanks called Chusok.

# What are the traditional foods of North Korea?

Rice and other grains are common in North Korea. People eat rice at almost every meal, including breakfast. They often make a sticky rice cake called *chaltok*. They also eat cooked cereals and porridge.

North Koreans enjoy many kinds of soups. They serve different soups for breakfast and dinner. In the summer, people in North Korea eat cold soups.

## Fact!

In North Korea, it is polite to slurp soup during meals.

*North Koreans eat rice and many kinds of kimchi.*

North Koreans eat many types of vegetables. They often make a pickled cabbage dish called kimchi. Most kimchi recipes include a salted sauce, red pepper, and garlic.

# What is family life like in North Korea?

Most North Koreans do not have time for large families. Women and men both work more than 40 hours a week. They must also attend political meetings. Children stay with grandparents or in day care while their parents work.

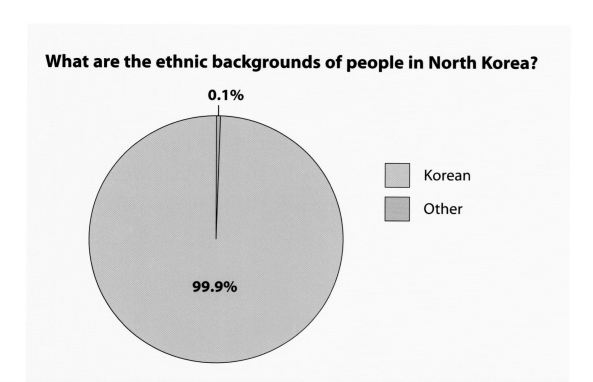

**What are the ethnic backgrounds of people in North Korea?**

0.1%

99.9%

Korean

Other

*A North Korean family celebrates May Day in Pyongyang.*

Many couples wait to have children. In North Korea, serving the country is more important than family life. All men must serve in the military for 10 years. Many women also join. Soldiers often get more money and food than other workers.

# North Korea Fast Facts

**Official name:**

Democratic People's Republic of Korea

**Land area:**

46,490 square miles (120,409 square kilometers)

**Average annual precipitation:**

40 inches (102 centimeters)

**Average January temperature:**

25 degrees Fahrenheit (minus 4 degrees Celsius)

**Average July temperature:**

75 degrees Fahrenheit (24 degrees Celsius)

**Population:**

22,466,481 people

**Capital city:**

Pyongyang

**Language:**

Korean

**Natural resources:**

coal, copper, fluorspar, gold, graphite, hydropower, iron ore, lead, magnesite, pyrites, tungsten, salt, zinc

**Religions:**

| | |
|---|---|
| Nonreligious | 68% |
| Traditional beliefs | 16% |
| Chongdogyo | 14% |
| Buddhism | 2% |

# Money and Flag

## Money:

North Korea's money is called the won. In 2004, 1 U.S. dollar equaled 2.2 won. One Canadian dollar equaled 1.66 won.

## Flag:

North Korea's flag has three bands divided by thin white stripes. The blue bands stand for peace and independence. The red band represents people who fought for North Korea's freedom. The star stands for the ideas of Kim Il Sung and the future of the country.

# Learn to Speak Korean

Korean is the official language of the people of North Korea. Learn to speak some Korean words using the chart below.

| English | Korean | Pronunciation |
|---------|--------|---------------|
| hello | an nyong ha seyo | (AHN YUNHG HAH say-OH) |
| good-bye | an nyonghi kaseyo | (AHN YUNHG-hee KA-say-OH) |
| please | jom | (JOHM) |
| thank you | kamsa hamnida | (kahm-SAH HAHM-nee-dah) |
| yes | yeh | (YEH) |
| no | aniyo | (AH-nee-yo) |

# Glossary

calligraphy (kuh-LIG-ruh-fee)—the art of drawing or painting words

ceramic (suh-RAM-ik)—having to do with objects made out of clay

communist (KOM-yuh-nist)—having to do with supporting communism; communism is a way of organizing a country so that all the land, houses, and factories belong to the government or community.

independent (in-di-PEN-duhnt)—free from the control of other people or things

manufacturing (man-yuh-FAK-chur-ing)—the process of making something

martial art (MAR-shuhl ART)—a style of self-defense and fighting

military (MIL-uh-ter-ee)—the armed forces of a state or country

mineral (MIN-ur-uhl)—a substance found in nature that is not made by a plant or animal

tram (TRAM)—a vehicle on rails used to carry passengers on city streets

# Internet Sites

FactHound offers a safe, fun way to find Internet sites related to this book. All of the sites on FactHound have been researched by our staff.

Here's how:
1. Visit *www.facthound.com*
2. Type in this special code **0736837566** for age-appropriate sites. Or enter a search word related to this book for a more general search.
3. Click on the **Fetch It** button.

FactHound will fetch the best sites for you!

# Read More

**Feldman, Ruth Tenzer.** *The Korean War.* Chronicle of America's Wars. Minneapolis: Lerner, 2004.

**Kummer, Patricia K.** *Korea.* Enchantment of the World. New York: Children's Press, 2004.

**Miller, Debra A.** *North Korea.* Modern Nations of the World. San Diego: Lucent Books, 2004.

**Parks, Peggy J.** *North Korea.* San Diego: Blackbirch Press, 2003.

# Index